The Caudills:
Courageous Missionaries

The Caudills:
Courageous Missionaries

TOM McMINN
Illustrated by Jack Woodson

1664

BROADMAN PRESS
Nashville, Tennessee

© Copyright 1982 • Broadman Press.
All rights reserved.
4242-77
ISBN: 0-8054-4277-4

Dewey Decimal Classification: J266.092
Subject headings: CAUDILL, HERBERT//CAUDILL, MARJORIE//
MISSIONS—CUBA
Library of Congress Catalog Card Number: 81-70474
Printed in the United States of America

To
My children—Sean and Shannon—
and to those children
who feel a special call to missions

Contents

Growing Up Days for Herbert 9

Marjorie's Prayers Are Answered 15

A Call to Missions 21

(Los) Primeros Años en Cuba (Early
    Years in Cuba) 29

Taking God's Word to People 35

Courage in Prison 43

Release from Prison 53

Important Dates in the Lives of Herbert
    and Marjorie Caudill 59

Remember? 61

About the Author 63

Growing Up Days for Herbert

"Hurry up, Herbert. It's almost time to leave for school," said Willie.

Herbert was busy at the kitchen table. He was practicing writing the alphabet letters. Papa was teaching him how to write, and Herbert wanted to do his very best.

"Just a minute. I need to try this letter one more time," shouted Herbert. He wrote very carefully, trying to make the letter just right. He finished, looked at the letters he had written, and smiled. He was pleased with what he had written.

Papa, who taught at the school, and Willie, Herbert's brother, were at the door, ready to leave.

Herbert hurriedly put on his jacket and grabbed his books. He enjoyed these walks to school. He liked having this time with his father. They could talk about things on the way to school.

"Herbert, keep up. Don't lag behind," called Papa.

Herbert was standing still, looking at some big oak and pine trees. He decided on a name for them.

"I'll call this place with the big oak and pine trees Chicago," Herbert said to Willie. Then he turned to his father. "I like the way you help me learn about

9

places, Papa. Do you think I'll ever travel to some of these places?'' asked Herbert.

Papa smiled and said, ''Herbert, if God wants you to live in a place, he will help you get there.''

When they got home after school, Willie and Herbert helped Papa with the chores. One of Herbert's jobs was to milk the cows before supper.

After the evening meal, Herbert got out his paper and asked his father to help him with his writing. Soon it was time for bed.

The next morning, Herbert woke up to see fresh snow on the ground. He jumped out of bed, hurried to get dressed, and ran into the kitchen. Mother was busy getting breakfast ready. Willie and Father were already at the table.

''Mother, have you looked outside?'' asked Herbert.

''Yes,'' answered Mother. ''Isn't the snow pretty? I guess you and Willie and Papa will ride in the buggy to school today.''

''Papa, can I drive the buggy?'' asked Herbert.

''We'll see later,'' said Papa. ''Now, eat a good breakfast.''

Soon they were on their way to school. Herbert was thinking about all the fun he was going to have playing in the snow at recess.

In the summer of 1915 when Herbert was in the seventh grade, the family moved to Cedartown, Georgia. Herbert's father was going to be the principal of the Benedict School. Herbert liked having his father for a teacher and principal.

In 1916, the family moved again—this time to Tift County, Georgia. Here they lived on a small farm.

Herbert's job was to help clear the land of pine trees. Herbert looked at the land and thought "There's a lot of work to do here. I'm tired of school. Maybe Papa will let me stay out of school for a while."

He ran back to the house to find Papa.

"Papa, Papa," Herbert called. "I need to talk to you. Where are you?"

Papa came in the back door to the house. "Slow down, Herbert. What's all this excitement?" he asked.

"Papa, there's a lot of work to do here. I think you need me to do more about clearing those pine trees. I want to stay out of school for a while. I could work here on the farm to help you," explained Herbert.

Papa thought about what Herbert said. Then he looked straight at Herbert and asked, "Herbert, are you sure you want to stay out of school?"

Herbert nodded his head. "Yes."

"All right, then," said Papa. "But if you decide to go back to school, that's OK, too."

Herbert stayed out of school one year and worked, clearing the land on the farm. In 1918, he enrolled at Tifton High School to continue his education.

"Herbert, Willie, it's time to go," said Papa. "We need to leave now so we won't be late for the meeting."

"Coming," shouted the boys.

When they arrived at the New River Baptist

11

Church, the choir was already singing a hymn. Papa and the boys sat down. Herbert enjoyed going to church with his father. Being with his father was always special.

During the revival service, Herbert listened to all that was said. He listened carefully to the preacher. He had heard words like this before. After all, he was fifteen years old. But tonight the words had a new meaning.

The time came for the invitation at the end of the sermon. The preacher asked for those who wanted to accept Jesus Christ as Savior to come down front. Herbert thought about what the preacher had said. He wanted to do this. He left his place in the pew and walked down to the front of the church. He accepted Jesus as his Savior.

At the close of the revival meeting, the preacher announced that these who had come forward during the services would be baptized in the creek soon.

Herbert was excited. He now knew Jesus in a personal way. He felt that God wanted him to do something special with his life.

The next morning Herbert went to work in the fields as usual. Only this morning, he took a Bible with him.

"Herbert, come sit with us for lunch," said his brother.

"No, thanks," said Herbert. "I've got some reading to do."

"What are you going to read?" asked Willie.

"I'm going to read through the Bible this summer."

12

"Good luck," said Willie.

Herbert sat down. He began to eat his lunch as he opened the Bible to Genesis. Before the summer was over, Herbert had read the Bible from Genesis to Revelation.

During the next several years, Herbert went to high school. He traveled five and one-half miles each way every day. In the spring of 1922, he graduated. During all this time, reading his Bible each day was an important part of his life.

Marjorie's Prayers Are Answered

It was a nice day in Belton, Texas. Marjorie Jacob was sitting on the steps to the front porch, thinking. "I really want to learn to play the piano," she thought. "I want to do this more than anything else in my life right now."

Marjorie remembered what her teachers at church had said. "Talk to God. Ask him to help you with all things in your life."

Marjorie bowed her head. "Dear God," she prayed, "I really want to play the piano. If you let me learn, I'll use my music to tell people about you."

A lot had happened in Marjorie's life since her birth in Little Springs, Mississippi, in 1908. The family had moved to Belton, Texas, where her father taught in the college.

In Belton, Marjorie began school. She enjoyed arithmetic, English grammar, and music. When she was eight years old, she attended a church camp. She remembered that camp because she learned to swim there.

Marjorie continued to think about music. She loved to sing and listen to records. One day her father came home. He looked for Marjorie.

"Marjorie, Marjorie," called her father. "I've got some good news for you."

"Coming Daddy," answered Marjorie. "What's the news?"

"You know how much you've really wanted to learn how to play the piano," said her father.

"Yes," said Marjorie, wondering what her father was going to say next.

"Well, I've talked to one of the students at the college. The student agreed to give you piano lessons as practice teaching. So, now you can study music."

"Oh, Daddy! Thank you," said Marjorie, with tears in her eyes. She was happy, for now she could learn to play the piano. This was a dream come true. This was a special surprise.

Later that night while Marjorie was in bed, she thought about her prayer to God asking him to help her learn to play the piano. She thanked God now for this opportunity. "God, thank you for letting me have piano lessons. Help me remember that I promised to tell other people about you with my music."

Meeting the student for the piano lessons would be easy. But finding a piano to practice on would be difficult for Marjorie. Marjorie's father did not receive a big salary as a college professor. There was no money to buy a piano. So Marjorie would have to look for a piano to practice on at the college.

Later in her life, Marjorie used her music to teach people to play the piano and to write songs in another language so people could hear about Jesus.

Soon, the Jacob family moved to Macon, Georgia. Moving was a sad occasion for Marjorie. Her piano

17

lessons would stop. Marjorie thought, "How can I continue learning to play the piano? Will there be a piano I can practice on at the new college where Daddy teaches?"

Marjorie's uncle came for a visit. He knew how much Marjorie wanted to learn to play the piano.

"Marjorie," he said. "You really want to play the piano, don't you?"

"Oh, yes!" said Marjorie.

"All right," he said. "If you will promise to practice very hard every day, I'll help you."

"Oh, wonderful!" said Marjorie, excitedly.

"Yes. I'll give you the money for the lessons if you can find someone to teach you."

"Oh, Uncle, thank you!" exclaimed Marjorie as she gave him a big hug. She was so excited she ran through the house shouting, "I'm going to play the piano!"

Again, God had provided a way for Marjorie to learn music. Marjorie soon met Mrs. Farrar, the wife of the dean of arts at Mercer University. Mrs. Farrar gave her piano lessons. Marjorie studied hard. Because Mercer did not have a music department, Marjorie had to look for a piano she could practice on. She had promised her uncle that she would practice. So she had to find a piano.

When they moved into the faculty apartments at Mercer University, Marjorie's father bought a piano. Now Marjorie would have a piano to practice on—a piano of her very own. However, there was a problem. Because they lived near other families in the apart-

18

ments, Marjorie had to find a time to practice when it would not disturb the others.

After graduating from high school, Marjorie continued her training in music by enrolling at Wesleyan Conservatory for Music on a two-year scholarship.

A Call to Missions

One Sunday evening in 1923 after the Christmas holidays, Herbert went to the Baptist Young People's Union meeting at the Tattnall Square Baptist Church. He enjoyed these times of fellowship. There was a crowd of young people in the room.

Across the big, black stove a pretty, blond girl noticed an attractive young man. The girl, Marjorie, leaned over to a friend and asked, "Who is that guy over there?"

"Oh, that's Herbert Caudill," her friend said. "He's from Tift County. He goes to Mercer. He's the one who puts wood and coal in the professors' offices for their stoves every morning. I think he also works in the school library."

Marjorie said, "Well, I want to meet him."

So the friend walked with Marjorie over to where Herbert was standing.

"Hello, Herbert. I want you to meet Marjorie Jacob," the friend said.

"Hello," said Herbert.

The friend went to talk with someone else in the room. Marjorie and Herbert were left to get better acquainted.

They enjoyed the meeting that night. Herbert

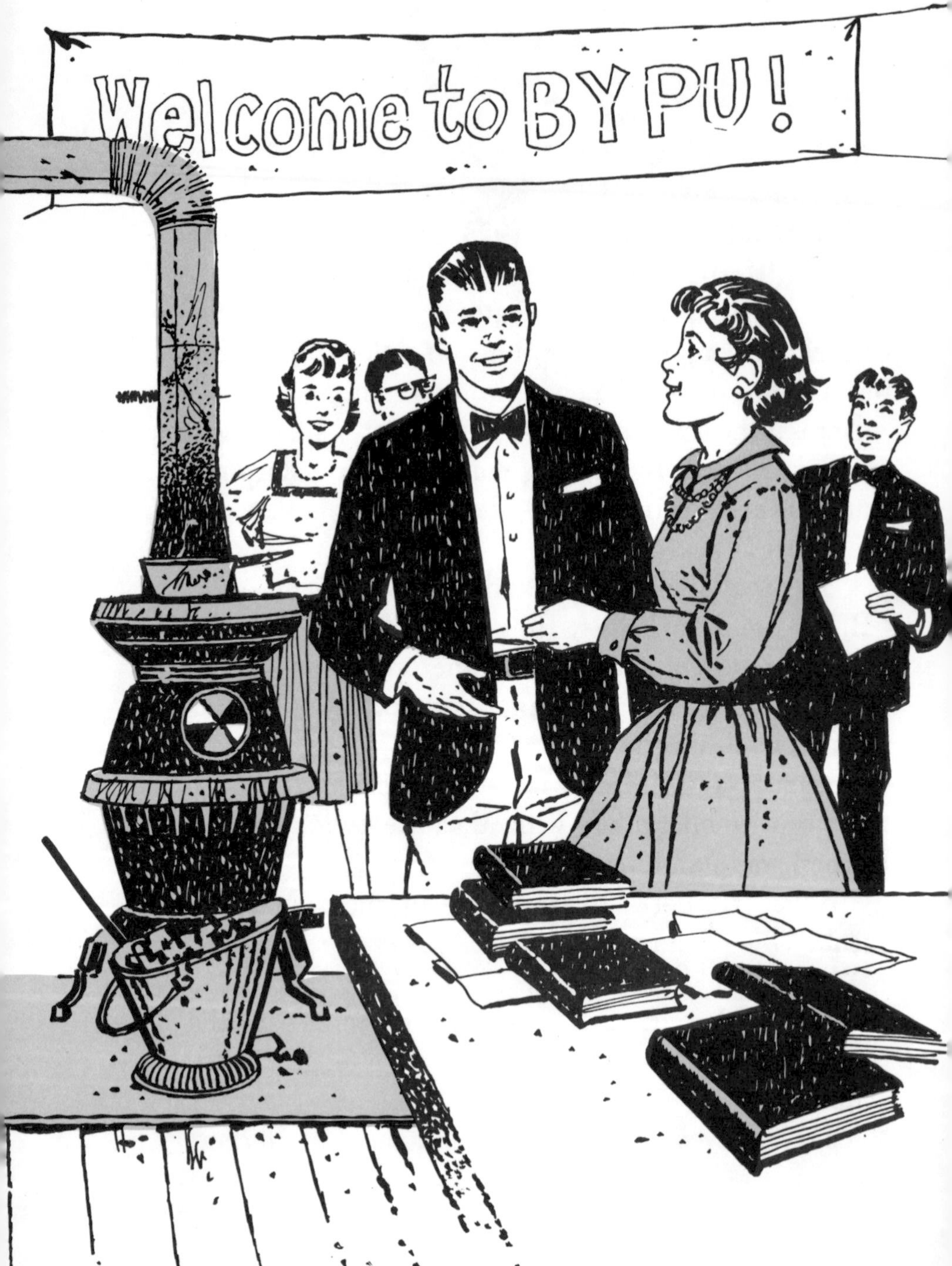
Welcome to BYPU!

called on Marjorie later in the week. This began the months of dating, long before Herbert graduated from Mercer.

At the awards assembly held at the end of his second year at Mercer, Herbert was awarded the medal for excellence in Greek. He had the highest grade in Greek in the entire school. Herbert received the award dressed in his working clothes. He had been gardening on the school grounds and had just come in to see who would receive awards. This award was a surprise to him.

In 1926, the Tattnall Square Baptist Church in Macon, Georgia, ordained Herbert to the gospel ministry, and he left for The Southwestern Baptist Theological Seminary in Forth Worth, Texas. Those were exciting days for Herbert.

While in seminary, Herbert never forgot Marjorie. They wrote many letters to each other.

During Herbert's time in seminary, God was preparing him for missionary service. Herbert was pastor of the Lexington Street Baptist Mission Church sponsored by the Gambrell Street Baptist Church. It was here that Herbert performed his first baptism.

Herbert enjoyed this mission work. He was feeling a special call to be a pastor.

In 1928, Herbert received his master of theology degree from Southwestern Seminary. He returned to Macon, Georgia, where he pastored four churches in the Middle Baptist Association and lived in Newington, Georgia.

During this time in Georgia Herbert began to feel a special call from God to mission service. At Thanksgiving in 1928, Walter Moore came to speak with Herbert. Walter was a pastor in Cuba and was in Screven County visiting his wife's family.

Walter said, "Herbert, you might like to come to Cuba. There are many churches there that need pastors."

"I don't know, Walter," said Herbert. "I like what I'm doing here. These people need a pastor, too."

"Well, you think about it," said Walter. "I'll keep in touch."

"OK," said Herbert. "I'll think about it. I want to do what God wants me to do."

Walter Moore returned to Cuba. He never forgot his talk with Herbert. Walter talked with Dr. M. N. McCall, who was the leader of Southern Baptist work in Cuba. Dr. McCall was very interested in Herbert. In 1929 Dr. McCall wrote a letter to Herbert.

> DEAR HERBERT,
>
> Reverend Walter Moore has shared with me the conversation he had with you on Thanksgiving of 1928. I am writing, hoping that you will feel led of God to join us in our work in Cuba.
>
> There is a great need for workers here. We need young men of your training and calling to help us minister to these people.
>
> Herbert, we need you. God needs you here. The English-speaking church in Havana needs a pastor. They need you. If you feel this is where God wants you to serve him,

please let me hear from you as soon as possible.

His servant,
Reverend M. N. McCall

Herbert read the letter again and again. He didn't know what to do. He felt that this might be what God wanted him to do. He thought of Marjorie. She had told him when they first started dating that she wanted to be a missionary. Would she consider marrying him and go to Cuba with him? Did she feel a call to missions in Cuba as he did?

Herbert spent time in prayer. He tried to find what God wanted him to do with his life. Soon, Herbert reached his decision. He would go. This was how God wanted him to live his life.

This decision meant leaving the United States. Leaving his family and friends would be hard. But God had called him to a special ministry of telling Cuban people about God's love. Herbert knew God would help him.

Now, Herbert had to find a way to tell Marjorie.

Herbert realized that Marjorie had never heard him preach. He invited her to come to the North Newington Baptist Church near Oliver, Georgia, for the services one Sunday. Marjorie accepted the invitation. She was excited about being with Herbert and hearing him preach. Marjorie had felt for a long time that God wanted her to share her life with Herbert. But she also wanted a career herself.

When Marjorie arrived at the church she was asked to play the piano for the worship service. She

gladly accepted the invitation, remembering her promise to God to use music to serve him.

After the worship service, Herbert took Marjorie to catch the train to return to Macon. They were waiting at the station when Herbert said, "Marjorie, I feel God calling me for a special kind of service. I feel that he wants me to go to Cuba."

Then Herbert waited for a response from Marjorie.

After a short time, Marjorie said, "Herbert, you know you have to do what God calls you to do. If it's Cuba, then, you need to go."

Herbert was excited about Marjorie's response, but he was nervous about what he wanted to ask her.

"Marjorie, how would you like to go to Cuba to work as a missionary? I want you to come with me. I want you to share my life. I want you to be with me in Cuba as my wife," said Herbert.

Herbert looked into Marjorie's eyes and asked, "Will you marry me, Marjorie Jacob?"

"Oh, Herbert," said Marjorie. "I promised God a long time ago that if he would help me learn music I would use the knowledge and skill to tell other people about him. Oh, Herbert, Cuba? Are you sure?" asked Marjorie.

"Yes," answered Herbert. "I plan to go this May. But, you go home and think it over. Don't answer now. Let me know in a week or two."

"So soon? I want to finish my college work at Mercer. Would I have time?" asked Marjorie.

"Yes, I'll go on to Cuba and return to Macon," said Herbert.

They talked until the train came. They both felt this was God's special calling for their lives. They were glad God could use them.

Marjorie's answer to Herbert's question was yes.

On May 23, 1929, Herbert Caudill arrived in Cuba to begin his ministry with the English-speaking Baptist church of Havana. The next year he returned to Macon, Georgia, where he and Marjorie were married in October, 1930.

On October 17, 1930, Marjorie and Herbert left Macon for a short honeymoon trip to Atlanta. Then they returned to Macon to get Marjorie's things together. On their way to Cuba, they stopped in West Palm Beach, Florida, for a brief visit with an aunt. Late in October, 1930, they arrived in Havana, Cuba.

Marjorie and Herbert knew they could face anything because they felt this special call from God to be missionaries. They knew God would be with them in the years ahead.

(Los) Primeros Años en Cuba
(Early Years in Cuba)

As soon as Herbert and Marjorie arrived in Cuba, they began learning the Spanish language. If they were to minister to the Cuban people, they had to learn to talk with them.

In January, 1931, Herbert and Marjorie began working with the first Spanish-speaking Baptist church in Calabazar. Marjorie was asked to be the church organist. Right away, God began to use her music talents.

Marjorie wanted to provide opportunities for children to learn about Jesus. So she organized a Sunbeam Band in Regla. During the years ahead, she translated the Sunbeam Band materials into Spanish, with the help of a daughter, Jane.

The work with children grew. Children began to bring other children with them. Soon, it was necessary to start a Girls' Auxiliary for older girls.

"Herbert," Marjorie said. "We need someone to lead the GA program. We just don't have anyone trained to do it."

"Yes, we really do need this work. Maybe I can lead the GA program," said Herbert.

"Yes," Marjorie said. "You know the work, and

the children respond so well to you. You're the perfect choice."

Well, OK," agreed Herbert. "When should I start?"

"How about next week? Check your calendar," said Marjorie.

So, GA work was started. Years later, in 1949, the first GA camp was held. Margaret, another daughter, was the camp director.

Soon, boys were coming, and a Royal Ambassadors program was started. From this early work with children in Cuba came future Cuban teachers and preachers. God was beginning to train others for his work in Cuba through the lives of Marjorie and Herbert Caudill.

In 1933, Marjorie returned to Georgia for the birth of her daughter, Margaret. Herbert joined Marjorie after the birth. During this time in Georgia, Herbert realized that Marjorie and the baby couldn't return to Cuba with him. There was no way they could live on sixty-five dollars a month as a family. Herbert was also concerned about the revolution going on in Cuba. Would it be safe to return?

When the Georgia Woman's Missionary Union learned about this problem, they decided to help. They knew God wanted Marjorie and Herbert in Cuba. So they said they would give money to the Caudills so they could continue to do God's work in Cuba. God, again, was providing a way for Marjorie and Herbert to tell people about Jesus.

As he was returning to Cuba, Herbert learned of shooting and violence in Havana. The ship he was traveling on had to wait at Key West, Florida. As he sat in the dining room of the ship, Herbert met one of the ship's officers. As they talked, Herbert noticed how often the officer used unnecessary bad language. The officer used God's name in a way that offended Herbert.

The officer looked at Herbert. He said, "Why are you going to Cuba? This is a bad time."

Herbert looked straight into the eyes of the officer and said, "I am a pastor of a Baptist church in Cuba. My people need me."

Immediately the officer realized what he had been saying and how he was using God's name. He changed the way he was talking. The officer did not use God's name in a bad way again while talking with Herbert.

This experience reminded Herbert of Psalm 19:14, "Let the words of my mouth, and the meditation of my heart, be acceptable in thy sight, O Lord, my strength, and my redeemer."

When Marjorie and Margaret returned to Cuba, Herbert asked that they be sent somewhere outside Havana to work. He said to Reverend McCall, "I feel that I need to get away from Havana where we have a lot of missionaries working. I feel Marjorie and I could be more useful away from the city. Can you assign me to some mission work somewhere outside of Havana?"

"Yes, Herbert, I can," answered Reverend McCall. "There is a church in Regla, across the bay from Havana, which needs a pastor."

32

"Great," said Herbert. "When would be a good time to leave for Regla?"

"Herbert, you need to know that this place is a rough fishing village. The people are a rough kind. There are unpleasant smells from the bay and a tanning factory near the town."

"I know we'll have to adjust, but let us try," pleaded Herbert.

"OK," said Reverend McCall. "I'll give you a few months."

Herbert and Marjorie lived in the fishing village for sixteen years. During this time Herbert pastored three churches at Regla, Guasimal, and the English-speaking church in Havana.

Taking God's Word to People

Marjorie knew that music could be a way to reach people. She felt the need for more English hymns to be in Spanish. So she began translating the hymn "I Know Whom I Have Believed" into Spanish.

Yo Sé a Quien Yo He Creído
(I Know Whom I Have Believed)

No sé por qué su gran amor
Mi Dios me reveló,
Y siendo yo tan pecador
Jesús me redimió.
Coro
Pero sé a quien yo he creído
Y estoy seguro que es poderoso,
Poderoso para aquel día
Mi depósito guardar.
2
Y no sé como esta fe
Jesús me impartió,
Ni como, al creer en El
Tan dulce paz me dió.
3
No sé como el Espíritu
Convence al pecador,
Y su palabra crea en él
La fe en el Salvador.

4

No sé la hora en que Jesús
Al mundo volverá,
Si moriré, o si en el aire
Me recibirá.*

God used this hymn in a special way to reach a young man named Mario. Mario lived in a small town in Cuba. He did not go to church. But Mario had a friend who went to a Baptist church. Mario liked his friend, even if he was a Protestant. Mario thought that Protestants were bad people.

"Mario," said his friend, "we are having special meetings at our church this week. Why don't you come with me?"

"Me? Go to church? No!" said Mario.

"Well, here, take this slip of paper. It tells you all about the meeting," said the friend. "I'll be there. If you decide to come, look for me."

Mario put the slip of paper in his pocket. He thought no more about it.

That night, Mario went to the corner of the street. He could see the church. His friend was there. But Mario couldn't go. He turned around and went down the street to a movie. Mario reached in his pocket and crushed the invitation to the revival meeting.

The next night, the same thing happened. Mario went to the church, but turned around and left.

*(In Spanish poetry final vowels are run together with initial vowels on the succeeding words, to be sung on the same note. These "running together places" are marked for anyone who wants to try to sing the Spanish words.)

On the third night, Mario felt he needed to go to the church to please his friend. He sat on a backseat with his friend. Mario listened to the music. The choir was singing the song Marjorie had translated, "I Know Whom I Have Believed." Mario listened carefully to the words of the hymn and to the sermon. He felt there was something missing in his life. When the invitation was given, Mario walked down the aisle of the church and told the preacher he believed that Jesus was his Savior.

Marjorie heard about what happened to Mario. She was glad God was using music to tell people about Jesus. Mario later became a pastor of a church in Cuba.

In 1935, a building program started in Cuba. The Baptist Temple Church in Havana was remodeled and a third story added. In November, classes were started for ministerial students. Herbert taught classes in Old and New Testament studies, church history, and religious education. During this time, Herbert was also pastor of the three churches.

Marjorie also taught in the seminary. She taught music classes to help train students to use music in the churches. During this time, Marjorie prayed to God saying she would teach piano to anyone who would use the music in the Lord's work. Soon, a ten-year-old girl from a small mission church came to her. The mission church had a piano, but no one knew how to play it. This young girl was willing to learn and would play for the worship services of the mission church. Marjorie agreed to teach the girl.

The young girl's mother came with the girl for the

piano lessons. Marjorie helped the girl understand the words of the songs. Soon, the girl accepted Jesus as her Savior. As the girl's mother listened, she too heard about Jesus. Marjorie gave the mother a Bible. Later, the mother accepted Jesus as Savior. God was using Marjorie's music to tell other people about Jesus.

One day, years later, Herbert decided to make a trip to the province of Las Villas. This would be a long trip. He had received a box of small Gospels and wanted to distribute the Gospels to the people. He invited a seminary student to go with him.

As they traveled, they came to a roadblock. A guard approached the car.

"We need to inspect the trunk of your car. Get out," said the guard.

Herbert got out of the car. He went around to the back of the car and opened the trunk. The guard inspected the trunk.

Then the guard looked in the backseat of the car. The guard looked at the Gospels on the seat. "What are these books?" he asked.

"These are Gospels given to me. I'd like to share one with you. Here, take one," said Herbert.

The guard took the Gospel. He opened the pages.

"Do you think your friends would like one, too?" asked Herbert as he grabbed a handful of Gospels and gave them to the guard.

"Move on," shouted the guard.

As they traveled, Herbert and the seminary student were stopped again and again. When it was possible, they gave Gospels to the guards. Some-

times the guards would allow them to give Gospels to people who were standing nearby.

The mission work continued. Even when it was hard, Herbert and Marjorie showed courage.

Because of the difficult times in Cuba, Marjorie and Herbert decided it would be best for their son, Herbert, Jr., to return to the United States. Diplomatic relations between Cuba and the United States had been broken. The Cuban government had closed the English-speaking high school, and many of the professors had returned to the United States.

With the help of friends in Cuba and Georgia, Herbert, Jr., returned to the United States to continue his education at the Berry School in Rome, Georgia, on January 26, 1961.

The day he left was a sad day for Marjorie and Herbert. They knew they might not see Herbert, Jr., for a long time.

Herbert and Marjorie were glad that Herbert, Jr.,

would have this opportunity. They also were thankful that their daughters, Margaret and Jane, were married and actively involved in telling other people about God's love.

Herbert and Marjorie remembered how their children had helped them in their work. Margaret had directed the first GA camp in Cuba. Jane began her own mission Sunday School when she was just nine years old and later helped to translate into Spanish the requirements for Queen with Scepter and Queen Regent.

Yes, their children had helped in the mission work. Herbert and Marjorie were thankful that God had blessed them in this good way. They were proud of their children.

Courage in Prison

As Herbert walked toward the chapel of the seminary in Havana, he could hear the music. Marjorie was leading choir practice for the Easter cantata to be presented at the annual convention of Cuban Baptists the next week.

Herbert walked in the door and went up to the group.

"I have some sad news to tell you," announced Herbert.

The room was quiet.

"I have just received word that Tomás, one of our pastors, has been arrested. I would like for you to join me as we pray for him and others who have been arrested."

The room was quiet as Herbert led the prayer. These were difficult days for the Baptist work in Cuba.

That night the house was quiet and still. Marjorie and Herbert were asleep. Suddenly, they were awakened by a loud knock at the door of their home.

Marjorie leaned over to Herbert and said, "Well, Herbert, they've come to get you." She and Herbert got out of bed to open the door.

Herbert went to the door and opened it. There

stood four armed, uniformed men. The men entered the apartment. They told the Caudills to sit on the couch and be quiet. For the next two hours, they searched the apartment.

After a while, the armed men began to search Herbert's desk. Marjorie did not want them to do that. She got up and went over to one of the men.

"Well, it looks like it is getting to be against the law to do religious work."

The armed man looked at Marjorie. "Oh, no, Señora," he said. "We're arresting your husband because he is a counterrevolutionary. He's working against the state."

Marjorie knew it was no use to talk. She went back to the couch and sat down with Herbert.

The armed men gathered personal papers, documents, and a package of Bibles. They took Herbert with them when they left the apartment at three o'clock in the morning.

Shortly after leaving the apartment, an armed man returned and said to Marjorie, "I need the keys to your car."

Marjorie gave the keys to the armed man. She knew the car would not be returned. She would now have to walk everywhere she went, ride the bus, or ask friends to take her where she needed to go. Times were going to be difficult, but God would give her the courage she would need to face the days ahead.

The armed men took Herbert to the Bureau of Investigation. Herbert was not allowed to take anything with him when he left the apartment. Herbert
44

was taken to a room at the entrance to the building. He saw other Cuban pastors in the room. They, too, had been arrested. All of them would soon have their pictures taken and be fingerprinted for government records.

The armed men led Herbert to a prison cell. He was placed in a cell by himself. Finally a lieutenant came to the cell and shouted at Herbert, "I want the keys to your office."

Herbert said, "I don't have the keys. My wife has the keys."

Herbert knew they would go and get the keys from Marjorie. He prayed that Marjorie would have courage during this difficult time.

The lieutenant returned to Herbert's cell.

"Which key is the key to your office?" demanded the lieutenant.

Herbert showed the lieutenant the key to his office. The lieutenant left, but returned shortly. He was angry with Herbert.

"I want to know how to get into the building where your office is. Which is the key to the building?" he demanded.

Herbert reached for the keys and said, "You need these two keys. The door has two locks."

Soon the guards moved Herbert to another cell. This second cell was not as nice as the first. Herbert stayed here for eight days. Several times he was called out for questioning.

Five days later, a guard came and took Herbert to a barbershop. He was given a fast shave. The captain of the guards came to Herbert.

46

"You are being given a special favor today," he said. "You will see your family. Don't tell them anything about what's happening to you here," he warned.

The captain continued, "Don't ask your family what is happening to them. Talk in Spanish. I'll be with you."

Herbert entered the room. There he saw Marjorie, Margaret, his daughter, and her children. Herbert visited with his family, holding his grandson. Marjorie looked at Herbert and asked, "Herbert, is there anything we can bring you?"

"Well, I don't have a towel, soap, toothbrush, or toothpaste. Oh, and I don't have a sheet or blanket. Bring me what you can," said Herbert.

Later that same day Marjorie came back to the prison with the things Herbert needed.

As Herbert was led away from his family, he asked the captain, "Where is my son-in-law, David Fite?"

"He is here with you," said the captain.

Herbert was surprised. He thought how hard it must be for Margaret with the children. Later Margaret told Herbert what she said to the boys.

"Daddy, it was so hard," said Margaret. "Mother called me the next morning and asked me what I was going to say to the boys. I had already thought through what I would say. I called them and said, 'Boys, we have been studying in our Bibles and in our mission studies how all through the years Christians have had to suffer for their faith. Now it is our time to suffer. The Communist

47

policemen took your daddy and your granddaddy to prison during the night.' "

The grandsons did not become bitter nor lose their faith. They knew their father and grandfather had come to Cuba to preach the gospel. They knew they would continue to do so in the prison, telling their fellow prisoners about Jesus.

Soon, Herbert was placed in a cell with other men. Some he knew. Tomás was in this cell. He said to Herbert, "Herbert, I found this piece of paper and this small pencil. Let's copy off a Bible passage."

"That's fine idea, Tomás," said Herbert.

"How about Psalm 27?" suggested Tomás.

The group of men in that prison cell wrote out on the little piece of paper the entire twenty-seventh Psalm from memory.

One day, right before mealtime, a guard called out, "Number 981. Get ready with all your belongings."

That was Herbert's number. He put all of his things in a blanket and got ready to leave. Guards took Herbert down to a car. There he saw his son-in-law, David Fite. Together they were taken to government offices. Later, they were taken to Cabaña Prison.

At the prison, Herbert and David were put in a cell with bars all around it. Soon, other pastors were put in the cell with them. After a while, Herbert and David were called out. They were taken to a big room that looked like a warehouse. Here they received prison uniforms, a jacket and pants.

From the warehouse room, Herbert and David

were taken to cell #12. The cells were like army barracks. Each cell was made to hold thirty-five people. But in cell #12, there were nearly two hundred prisoners. The beds were bunk beds with one bed on top of the other, four levels high. Some men had to sleep on the floor.

In cell #12, a man approached Herbert.

"Hi. I'm José. You remember me?" he asked.

Herbert looked at the man.

"You were in my home many years ago," said the man.

Now, Herbert remembered. In January 1938 Herbert had been in this man's home to tell others about Jesus. He had spent the night in the home of José.

José continued speaking to Herbert. "I told some of the other pastors here that if you were brought in, I wanted you to have my bed."

Herbert smiled at José, who was about fifty years old. This man wanted to sleep on the floor so Herbert could have a bed.

José shared food with Herbert until Herbert's food package arrived two weeks later.

All the time Herbert was in prison, Marjorie continued to pray for him and the other pastors. She told everyone to pray. She thought about Herbert all the time. These were difficult days for Marjorie.

She could not eat and began to lose weight. She sat and thought, "What can I do to help get Herbert out of prison? What can I take him that he would like to have?"

There was a knock at the door. Marjorie went to

the door. There stood several seminary students.

"Mrs. Caudill, we know you are worried about your husband. We just wanted to know if there is anything we can do for you," said the students.

"Oh, thank you. But I can't think of anything right now," said Marjorie.

One of the students said to Marjorie, "We heard you are not eating. We thought maybe you would like to come and eat meals with us at the seminary."

"Oh, you are so kind. I just don't know," said Marjorie.

"But we really mean it, Mrs. Caudill," the students replied.

"Well, all right, I'll come. It would be nice to be with someone at meals," Marjorie said.

The students told stories during meals to help Marjorie think of other things besides Herbert in prison and eating her meals. It worked. Soon Marjorie was eating and gaining back her weight.

One day Marjorie went to a women's meeting. There she told the women that she was saving her flour ration to make Herbert a cake. The women wanted to help, and they gave Marjorie their flour rations to make a small cake for Herbert. When Marjorie took the cake to Herbert, she told him how the women helped.

On May 14, Herbert went to trial. He was charged as being the chief leader of a band of conspirators against the Cuban government. His sentence was ten years in prison. Herbert was led away to begin serving his prison sentence.

During the days in prison, Herbert continued to

have trouble with his eyes. The doctors said he had a detached retina. As the days went by, Herbert lost the sight in his left eye and almost all the sight in his right eye.

Through friends in prison, he sent word to Marjorie. She immediately began to seek medical help for Herbert. She also began to try to get Herbert released from prison.

Release from Prison

"Herbert Caudill, with all his belongings!" the guard called out.

"This is it, Herbert," said a fellow prisoner. "You're going to be freed."

Herbert was sitting on a bunk talking with a few prisoners. He was not expecting this call from the guard. He thought, "Am I really going to be released from prison?"

Herbert, with the help of other prisoners, gathered up his belongings. There wasn't much to gather. With two small packages, Herbert said farewell to the prisoners and went with the guards.

The guards took Herbert to the storeroom where he had received his prison uniform on May 11, 1965. It was now eighteen months and fourteen days later.

A man looked at Herbert and said, "Take off those clothes. You will not need them anymore."

As Herbert took off his prison clothes, the man gave him a shirt and trousers to wear.

"You may leave some of your things for David Fite, if you want," said a guard. Herbert was glad to help David. He looked through his two small packages and got out some food and sheets which he left for David.

The guards took Herbert to the office of the La Cabaña prison. Here they returned an envelope to him containing his personal belongings which were taken when he entered the prison. Among the belongings in the envelope was a small Bible which Marjorie had tried to bring to Herbert while he was in prison.

Herbert was then taken by car to the Bureau of Investigation. As he followed the guards, he was led to a room. Upon entering the room, he saw Marjorie and a good friend with a captain in charge of release.

The captain explained to Herbert, "Mr. Caudill, you are being put under the custody of your wife, Marjorie. This will allow you to get the medical treatment needed for your eye."

> *Delivery of Prisoner*
> *****In the Department of Security of the State, it being the 14:00 hour of the day, twenty-fifth of November of one thousand nine hundred and sixty-six, "YEAR OF SOLIDARITY," giving fulfillment of what has been decreed by the Chief of this office or department there is carried out the delivery to Mrs. MARJORIE JACOB of the prisoner HERBERT CAUDILL WALTERS, who was condemned in the case 697/64 for 10 years of prison. Revolutionary Tribunal #1, District of Havana. Crime: Against the Integrity and Stability of the Nation. *****This procedure of liberty has the character of provisional until the Commission of Authorization of Conditional Liberty may receive all the documentation which at this time are in the process of being carried out.*
> *Horacio Carracedo*
> *J'Visit-Polit. DSE*

The Baptist friend led Marjorie and Herbert to his car. He drove them to the seminary garage where several students and professors were waiting. The group went to the seminary chapel for a short time of praise to God and prayers of thanksgiving. The day was November 25, 1966.

Several days later, the captain visited Herbert in his apartment at the seminary.

"Mr. Caudill," said the captain. "You may now take the necessary steps to leave this country."

"Thank you, Captain," replied Herbert. "But is there any word about David Fite's release?"

"None," answered the captain.

"Marjorie and I feel we cannot leave Cuba until David's release," continued Herbert. "We cannot leave our daughter, Margaret, and her three boys."

"I will check on this matter for you," said the captain.

Days passed. No word came about David.

Ring! Ring! Ring!

Herbert moved across the room and picked up the telephone receiver.

"Hello, Daddy. It's David. I'm home for a six-hour visit. Can you and Mother come over?"

"Thank God!" said Herbert. "Great news!"

A guard was with David at his home when Herbert and Marjorie arrived. The guard stayed in the background so the family could visit and speak privately.

Days later, David was released, and the family made final plans to leave Cuba. They would only be allowed to carry two small suitcases with them. It would be difficult to decide what to take with them and what to leave behind.

On the morning of February 7, 1969, Herbert,

Marjorie, David Fite, and his family left Cuba with their suitcases. They flew to Matamoros, Mexico, before arriving in Atlanta, Georgia.

The Capitol View Baptist Church of Atlanta offered their missionaries' home to the Caudills those first days as they adjusted to being back in the United States. They lived there until they settled back into life in the United States.

Herbert and Marjorie moved into their own home in the Atlanta area in June, 1969. They continue to serve God by speaking at churches and camps in the United States.

God used Herbert and Marjorie Caudill because they were willing to do God's will. They did what God wanted them to do. They were missionaries with courage.

Important Dates in the Lives of Herbert and Marjorie Caudill

Herbert's birth: August 17, 1903

Marjorie's birth: March 7, 1908

Herbert's conversion: 1918

Marjorie's conversion: 1917

Herbert's baptism: 1918

Marjorie's baptism: 1917

Herbert's ordination: 1926

Herbert began mission work in Cuba: May 23, 1929

Marjorie began mission work in Cuba: October, 1930

They began ministry with Spanish-speaking congregation: 1931

Herbert became professor at Baptist Seminary in Havana: 1935

Herbert became superintendent of Southern Baptist Home Mission Board work in Cuba: 1947

Herbert was arrested in Cuba: April 8, 1965

Herbert was released from prison: November, 1966

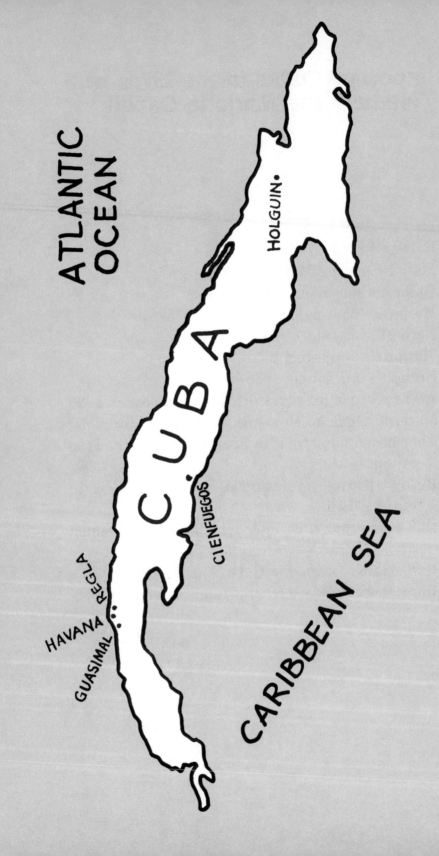

ATLANTIC
OCEAN

CUBA

HOLGUIN•

CIENFUEGOS

REGLA

HAVANA

GUASIMAL

CARIBBEAN SEA

Remember?

Herbert and Marjorie Caudill served God as missionaries for many years. They knew from early days in their lives that God wanted to use them in a special way. Think back to what you have read about the lives of these courageous missionaries. Try to answer these questions as you remember.

How did God prepare Marjorie and Herbert for service as missionaries? (See chapters 1 and 2.)

When did Herbert first hear about Cuba? (See chapter 3.)

What kinds of work did Marjorie and Herbert do as missionaries? (See chapters 4 and 5.)

What problems did Marjorie and Herbert have in doing what God wanted them to do? (See chapters 5 and 6.)

How did Marjorie and Herbert know God wanted them to be missionaries?

How can you tell God wants you to be a missionary?

What can you do to prepare you to be a missionary?

You may think God wants you to be a missionary. If so, talk with your family, your teachers at church, or your pastor. Share with them what you are thinking. They will be glad to help you. Ask them to pray for you as you try to find out what God wants you to do with your life.

Remember: Before you can tell other people about Jesus, you first need to accept him as your Savior. Pray to God and ask him to show you what he wants you to do. If you feel God is wanting you to make a decision now, talk with your teachers at church, your family, or your pastor.

About the Author

Tom McMinn lives in Brentwood, Tennessee, with his wife, Gayle, his son, Sean, and his daughter, Shannon. He is a member of Brentwood Baptist Church, where he teaches children in Sunday School.

Mr. McMinn works at the Baptist Sunday School Board in Nashville, Tennessee. He travels to many places to help teachers know how to teach boys and girls in Sunday School. He has written one book, *Prophets: Preachers for God.* He also writes teaching tapes and filmstrips to help boys and girls learn about God.

Date Due

Code 4386-04, CLS-4, Broadman Supplies, Nashville, Tenn., Printed in U.S.A.